T0150547

What if Mistakes Were Productive?

A Buddhist Perspective on Guilt

Other Works by this Author

What if Mistakes Were Productive?
A BUDDHIST PERSPECTIVE ON GUILT

Anila Trinlé

Translated from the French by Jourdie Ross

The Knowledge Workshop

RABSEL
PUBLICATIONS

ORIGINAL TITLE:
Et si l'erreur était fertile ?
©Rabsel Editions 2017

Special thanks from the translator to Marjorie Erickson.

RABSEL PUBLICATIONS
16, rue de Babylone
76430 La Remuée, France
www.rabsel.com
contact@rabsel.com

Rabsel Publications, La Remuée, France, 2021
ISBN 978-2-36017-041-8

Table of Contents

Preface

I met Anila Trinlé more than twenty years ago. She was not yet a
Buddhist nun at that point in time and was a volunteer accompanying patients at the Palliative Care Unit at the Paul Brousse
Hospital in Villejuif where I worked as a psychiatrist. It is an exceptional place where the staff does everything in their capacity
to enable those at the end of their lives to bring their existences
to a close in the best conditions; the staff eases patients' pain and
keeps their symptoms under control to the greatest extent possible. Nevertheless, in this place of final moments of life, at times
suffering is not so much in the body as in the heart. Often, the
weight of regret—things done and not done, said and not said—
stagnates there. With the grief and remorse that they could have

written their story differently, guilt sometimes possesses the mind and torments people to their last breaths.

How many times did Anila hear these regrets while at people's sides? Those lost opportunities to say something or to forgive, those *if onlys* that might have made all the difference between peace and the bitter taste of a relationship damaged forever that death no longer allows the time to repair? I have the intuition that this experience in palliative care gave Anila a well-honed insight into the impact of guilt on a human life. The roots of her authenticity are evident when she speaks to us with so much depth and humanity. She shares with us this knowledge that she acquired among those whose existences are coming to a close, as well as her own life experience that—like all human beings—is not free from mistakes, tangents, and regrets.

In this beautiful book that she offers us today, Anila connects the river of her personal journey with the majestic flow of the Buddha's teaching, bringing together her own reflections with this inexhaustible source of wisdom. The Buddha's teaching is demanding. Precision is required to understand it. Detailed and subtle knowledge of the concepts the Buddha entrusted to us is a component of the dimension of *wisdom*. This understanding then develops into the nondiscursive knowledge that arises from meditation. On this basis—in the space of trusting abandon that meditation opens—we are able to let this knowledge sink into us, to go beyond even logic and willpower. Clarity—ultimate under-standing of the Buddha's teaching—emerges from the meeting of these two worlds of knowledge. This clarity becomes evident in the appropriateness of our thoughts, our speech, and our actions that embody our *compassion* at work in the world. For is not the union of Wisdom and Compassion the essence of the spiritual path, as the great masters teach us?

As a Westerner, a mother, and a courageous woman who has been through the storms of life, Anila Trinlé sheds light on the concepts of regret, error, and guilt, which are often unclear to us. She gives us a clear and intelligible explanation of the at times complex and difficult-to-grasp ideas of the Buddha's teaching. In her words, they become accessible and transparent—directly applicable in our daily lives.

As a psychiatrist, I am too often confronted with the suffering generated by guilt not to recognize the relevance of this book. Our world needs such writing—to find other paths than those that society offers in the face of suffering based on guilt. To point out other paths of easing this pain, other ways of honoring who we are—free from the low self-esteem—or even self-hatred—that guilt feeds on.

Anila Trinlé gives us precious keys. Let us soak in her teaching. It needs time to saturate us in order to reveal its true color, its true depth. It is up to us to open the door and walk the path.

For, as the Buddha said, "I cannot give you enlightenment. You alone can do that."

So, why wait?

Give yourself this greatest gift!

Christophe Fauré[1]

---

[1] Psychiatrist, psychotherapist, and grief specialist. He has published numerous works on the subject with Albin Michel Publishing (in French).

Introduction

Our feelings of guilt exist in dependence on our relationship to making mistakes. We encounter these feelings—which are a source of suffering and relational difficulty—often and in any given situation. Whether there is factual guilt or not, this suffering can occur and lead us to lose confidence in ourselves and develop low self-esteem.

In the Buddha's teaching, the Dharma, there is no explanation or presentation of guilt. Not that Buddhists do not experience feelings of guilt, but rather the way that the Buddhist perspective deals with emotions or afflictions offers another approach. Furthermore, the notion of inherently immoral errors—an emotional consequence of our relationship to making mistakes—does not appear in the Dharma.

It is important to remember that the Buddha emphasized those parts of our way of functioning that hinder clarity of mind. He focuses on the afflictions—the primary harmful states of mind: desire-attachment, aversion, mental opacity, jealousy, and pride. We will delve deeper into these emotions and their functioning, and we will see why they are sources of dissatisfaction and unhappiness.

From a Buddhist point of view, the feeling of guilt is an amalgam of several of these afflictions: attachment to our mental representations of things, aversion to what has happened, mental opacity in that we only perceive situations based on our often limited representations, and, lastly, pride because without that where did we get the idea that we should never make mistakes?

Presenting guilt this way allows us to realize that the key is seeing our way of functioning for what it is: a process of identification with various constituents that we will explore in the next chapter.

The most important part of this reflection centers on our relationship to mistakes and their consequences. We would be so happy not to make mistakes! But is it possible? Our way of functioning is the cause of our mistake-making—a fundamental cause that is inherent to the process of identification with our body, our sensations, our emotions, and all that develops from there.

We judge the discrepancy between what happened and what should have happened, which we discover after the fact, to be an error. The Buddhist approach considers the idea of immorality to be the result of a negative judgment of our mistakes. They can be cognitive errors—mistakes arising from an incomplete evaluation of a given situation—or emotional errors due to getting carried away by an emotion without realizing it. It all happened so fast, and we couldn't see the consequences of our behavior until afterward.

If I had known, I would have; I should have seen; I shouldn't have reacted like that...such thoughts reveal our difficulty in taking responsibility for not having been right. What I'd like to emphasize here is the use of the conditional in all these phrases. Conjugation can sometimes help us better see what escaped us. If we are using the conditional, then it is evident that not all the conditions were present to act any other way! We would have liked for things not to have happened like that. In the moment, we acted the best we could have based on the evaluation in that instant. There's no doubt that our imagined best could indeed be perfect, but is that a reason to judge ourselves so severely and inflict the suffering of feeling guilty?

Looking at this, we can see that feelings of guilt arise based on the judgment of a mistake, and that they occur following a later evaluation of the situation. This is an important aspect that we will clarify.

We will carry out this reflection based on various aspects of the Buddha's teaching. Though the Dharma does not discuss guilt, we can find the elements necessary to work on these feelings in the teachings, and, little by little, we can train in resisting the habit of negative judgment that invalidates us.

Mistakes are an inherent part of the learning process, and no doubt we can become wise learners if we accept this!

In our culture, forgiveness is the response to guilt. It is healing and helps ease our suffering. Nevertheless, forgiveness also affirms the idea of moral judgment, a notion that is likewise absent in the Buddhist approach. We act and react in a limited and often mistaken way due to our way of functioning based on representations and afflictions. This is why it is important to consider these errors as inherent to our view of things—in order to be able to better see them and to cultivate the means to free ourselves from them.

The idea is not to reject our afflictions but rather to learn to relate to them differently when we see the consequences that they have on us and others. Using the three trainings, we can learn to no longer depend on these afflictions and to develop a kind and discerning state of mind. The three trainings are ethical action, meditation, and discernment. The Buddha taught these three essential methods so that we could liberate ourselves from our current condition.

Let us accept that we are imperfect! By calmly observing our way of functioning and becoming aware of our imperfections, we can transform them. As Gendun Rinpoche[2] said,

"An unseen flaw remains a flaw. A flaw one has seen is a potential strength."

This is certainly an inspiring approach, and also a source of joy! We can rejoice that we have seen an imperfection, that we are aware of an error. We can interrupt the tendency of blaming ourselves and make the path more productive.

---

2   A great meditation master who was sent to the West by the 16th Karmapa to develop Dhagpo Kagyu Ling and to create and direct retreat centers and monastic and lay hermitages in order to make the Dharma accessible for all.

The View of the Individual

To start, we will explore our way of functioning. Several perspectives will intersect and enrich each other in order to help us better understand what, in our way of interacting with our environment, leads us to experience guilt in a painful way.

The Buddhist Approach

When we say or think *me*, we are facing a paradox because we have the feeling that this *me* truly exists, yet if we look for it, we cannot find it. Where is this *me* that is at the heart of our experiences? Is it in my body? Is it in the brain? What knowledge do we have of this *me* that is both so familiar and yet so unknown? *Me*—is it the ego? What is the ego?

Buddhist psychology looks at this *me* in terms of self-grasping, a process of identification with various elements. We are a body endowed with a mind. We are knowing beings—that is one of our essential characteristics. This capacity to know allows us, on the one hand, to know ourselves, to know others, and to know our environment, and, on the other hand, it allows us to constantly acquire new knowledge, notably the means to clarify our minds.

How do we know, or how do we acquire knowledge?

When we see an object, a chair for example, our eye captures this image. Our vision, which is associated with several functions of the mind, identifies this image as a chair—my chair that I am especially fond of. Several mental factors come into play to apprehend and identify what the eye has perceived. Contact with the object generates sensation. The sensation can be experienced immediately as pleasure or displeasure, pleasant or unpleasant. Then distinction intervenes to identify the object's characteristics. This allows us to recognize the object: it's a chair. In our example, attachment takes hold—it's *my* chair, and it is my capacity for selective attention that decides this. Through this example, we can see that knowledge of this object occurs via the visual organ, sensation, distinction associated with emotions, and cognitive capacity, what we call consciousness.

This is the site of self-grasping, a process of identification with these five aggregates[3] of the body, sensations, distinctions, states of mind, and consciousness. This process of identification leads us to experience these various elements as a whole: *me*. From the moment that this *me* exists, *other* also exists.

We perceive ourselves as a lasting and independent entity, while we are, in fact, compound, interdependent, and impermanent. Our body is an amalgam of bones, muscles, viscera, blood, etc. Every part is itself made up of smaller parts, and, based on this collection of aggregates, we experience a whole.

As everything that is assembled one day comes apart, our body itself is impermanent. We are impermanent, and what we are today is the result of a multitude of causes and circumstances. In order for us to be alive today, of course, we needed two parents, but, additionally, many other people who contributed to our education, our good health, our material comfort, etc.

If we observe our sensations, we can see just how fleeting and transient they are. We move ceaselessly from one feeling to another, from one state of mind to another, from one emotion to another. And yet, at the heart of our experience, we have the feeling of something lasting, of certain and undeniable existence. In-

---

3   In this context, *aggregate* refers to the fact that all phenomena are composite. Each aggregate is made up of multiple elements.

tellectually, we know that these experiences are ephemeral, but on the level of feeling, at the very moment when we experience them, *we are* anger, sadness, or joy. *We are* the sensation of pleasure or the unpleasant feeling. And yet, all of these states of mind are unstable, impermanent, and dependent on the circumstances we encounter.

Our very existence is the result of interdependence, as is the entirety of our environment. We cannot find any entity that exists in a lasting way dissociated from everything else. We cannot find a single thing that has always been there, autonomous and immutable. When we become aware of this, we also become aware of how great a disparity there is between our habitual perception of ourselves and our environment and reality.

What we take to be *reality* is our version—our vision—of reality. It is in fact, *our* reality, and we put ourselves at the center of this reality, at the center of our world. As we have seen, our mode of acquiring knowledge is emotional and afflictive. Emotion is constantly present and accompanies our relationships to others and ourselves. In Tibetan, emotion is *nyeunmong*, which literally translates to *that which veils and generates suffering.* In order to have a term that is close to the meaning, this word is commonly translated as *disturbing emotion* or *afflictive* (*nyeun*: suffering) *obscuration* (*mong*). Emotion obscures and affects our perception of the world and others.

It is important to emphasize that the Buddha taught those things necessary for walking the path and realizing enlightenment. Buddhism is a soteriological path, in other words, a path of liberation. The description of a human being's way of functioning that the Buddha laid out specifically focuses on the inherent qualities of mind as well as those elements that maintain our unhappiness. This is why the teachings only catalogue the afflictions that act as obstacles and prevent us from reaching our goal. There are three fundamental afflictions: desire-attachment, aversion, and mental opacity or ignorance. Ignorance is not only the fact of not knowing, it is more specifically not perceiving reality as it truly is.

We can summarize the Buddhist view of human beings and our way of functioning like this: based on what we perceive, we acquire knowledge, and we experience our environment and ourselves based on mental representations colored by various afflictions. We think that we are in contact with reality, when in fact we are in contact with our own representations of reality.

The Western Approach

The Western approach is rich in definitions of the ego. Great thinkers have long theorized about what the ego is, how it functions, how it comes into existence, and its development. One of the ways of defining the ego is, first, a disposition to conceive a coherent self based on images of oneself and, second, an ability to manage, organize, and interact with the world, others, and ourselves in an appropriate way.

This adaptive ability allows a child to develop over time. In order to survive, a child needs to be loved, to feel loved and considered, and to be taken into account. This is essential for their safety and stability. Children respond with great intelligence to a wide range of situations in order to preserve their connection to the parent figure. The result of this effective adaptability becomes their identity, their character. Even if this adaptation is no longer necessary because the circumstances have changed, the adult that they have grown into will continue to react to the different circumstances they encounter based on their construction as a child.

Consider the example of a young boy who experiences his mother's lack of availability as a form of abandonment. He may use physical force, anger, and constant demands to get her attention—or, on the contrary, if he is not in touch with his own value, he may do everything he can to become invisible so as not to disturb her. In our somewhat simplified schema, he may establish a vindictive, authoritarian personality or a weak, unstable, and fearful personality. Both include the consequence of a lack of self-confidence.

This lack of confidence is likely marked by a feeling of guilt for not having *known* how to maintain the interest of his parent figure. This is, of course, a way of living and a way of interpreting his relationship to his mother. A child's needs may be quite far removed from their parent's capacities in one way or another.

A child may need a continual expression and show of love, while their mother may be reserved and not very skilled at sharing her feelings for various reasons related to her own personal history and character. Or, by contrast, the mother may have a need to be close to her child, showing a lot of tenderness and curiosity toward him, while the child, based on his own deeper character, may not be inclined toward this type of behavior.

The problem is not so much about an excess or absence of attention but rather about unsatisfied needs and expectations on the part of both child and parent. It would be incorrect to think that solely parental behavior leads to lack of self-confidence and feelings of guilt in a child. We can easily observe the degree to which each child's personality is singular.

We can define a child's character as the result of genetic transmission, the expression of familial temperament, and/or the impact of their education. Social, emotional, and cultural environment also have a large influence on a child's development. Likewise, the arrival of a sibling, the parents' separation, or a death in the family leave lasting imprints and mark a child's character.

The key point to retain is certainly that a child is very sensitive to their family and emotional environment. The love and attention those close to them show greatly influences their emotional construction. Likewise, difficult events that occur for a child and their family, along with happy and productive circumstances, have an effect on their development.

The Singularity of Each Being

While also accepting this approach, the Buddhist tradition explains the singularity of each child with a different view. A metaphor can help us understand in a simple way how tendencies, emotional potential, and, therefore, ways of representing one's environment and dealing with diverse situations are already present in the mind from birth.

The mind is a like a traveler who moves from hotel to hotel. This body, which is yours, is your mind's hotel for this life.[4]

If we extrapolate from this metaphor, we can consider that this voyager has baggage, and their baggage is filled with various components. If we observe several children, we can see how much their behavior differs in similar situations. For example, some will take a natural interest in ants, while others will ignore them, and yet others will play at trying to crush them.

---

4   Paraphrased from *The Thirty-Seven Practices of Bodhisattvas* by Gyalse Thogme Zangpo.

Child Development

Even if their behavior differs, children's development during their early childhood is very similar. A newborn has only a very fragmented perception of their mother. She is face, a nourishing breast, hands, a voice—without being a completely separate individual. Furthermore, for a newborn, their own body and that of their mother are a single whole—there is no differentiation between them.

A child begins to feel a difference between themself and their mother around seven or eight months old. This differentiation is a progressive process. Initially, mother and newborn are a single entity for the baby, and then progressively the child begins to see itself as separate from its mother. Though the notion of self is innate in the Buddhist tradition, over the course of a child's development, the construction of an *I* evolves and deepens.

However, several more years must pass before a child matures beyond perception involving the belief that their every thought, wish, and uttered expression has an effect on their environment. If a child thinks that their little brother is taking too much of their mother's attention and, in a moment of jealousy, wishes for him to disappear, and if the little brother indeed gets sick or dies, the older sibling will feel guilty for being responsible for their family's suffering.

A young child confuses the subjective universe with the objective universe. This is the age of magical thinking. It takes time to fully go beyond this way of grasping reality. A child only develops more distance in their relationship to their environment around five to seven years old.

However, a child's personality develops from birth based on the contents of their baggage, as we discussed earlier. A certain amount of self-confidence is necessary to go out and discover the world. If a child's environment has sufficiently nourished them—fulfilled their needs in terms of parental love and attention, the child finds an inner balance that allows them to face the external world with confidence in an environment that they perceive to be safe.

If their perception of the love and attention that their parents offered does not correspond to their needs, there may be a lack of confidence, leading to a lesser or greater tendency toward feeling guilty. Furthermore, an overly strict upbringing can reinforce low self-esteem or damage the feeling of security, and a child then becomes susceptible to a lack of self-confidence.

The problem is that a young child will take on the full responsibility for not being good enough, not being worthy of being loved—not being lovable in the literal sense—in order to retain the love and attention of their parents. This feeling may strongly condition their adult life. Low self-worth and lack of self-confidence inevitably lead to worsening self-esteem, which is fertile ground for guilt.

Dealing with this subject is always delicate. It would be incorrect to look for *the* individual whose fault it is. In reality, this occurs based on the meeting of multiple circumstances associated with our limited and emotional perception and the situations we encounter that are the basis for our representations.

In most cases, parents give their children love and attention. They do their best to give them a decent education. There are, however, cases of obvious mistreatment, and the consequences are sometimes extremely serious for the children. Mistreatment can have different faces—on both psychological and physical levels.

We have covered how important the first years of life are in determining the construction of an individual's personality, but we must also remember that it is the result of, first, the circumstances we encounter, and, second, the way that we understand, approach, and deal with those circumstances that more profoundly nurtures our principal character traits.

In the same way, throughout our entire lives, the representation that we have of a situation is the result of the tendencies we have nourished and accumulated over time, as we only have access to our own version of reality. In addition, this representation conditions our response to our situation, which further reinforces our representation. Fortunately, this functioning is not irremediable. Numerous instructions on the Buddhist path allow us to remedy it. We will delve further into this in the following chapters.

Our Relationship to Making Mistakes

The relationship that we establish with our mistakes will have a great influence on our feelings of guilt. But what is a mistake? The dictionary proposes the definition: *an act or judgment that is misguided or wrong.*[5] From a Buddhist perspective, a question naturally arises upon reading this definition, "Isn't being wrong inherent to our way of functioning?"

Is it possible not to be wrong in our evaluations, our reactions, and our understanding of the diverse situations that we encounter? How could we be right in every situation if we only have access to our own perception of reality—our own reality?

---

5   Oxford Languages

Nevertheless, we imagine, more or less consciously, that we should always react in a relevant and appropriate way. As soon as our errors appear before us, judgment arises and invalidates our response to the situation. I should have known; I should have seen; I shouldn't have done such and such.

It's Peter's first day in a new position at work. He got a promotion, and he wants to show he's up to the job. A little stressed and worried, he starts to go through the files in progress. One of the files has an *urgent* stamp on it. Without waiting a moment longer, he consults the file and begins brainstorming possible solutions. He takes his time, studying the different aspects of the case, deepening his reflection without noticing the time passing. It slips his mind that he has a meeting with his new boss. Suddenly, he sees his boss appear at the door of his office, looking surprised and a bit irritated at having been made to wait. At that moment, a feeling of unforgivable error washes over Peter and the feeling of guilt overtakes him. "How could I forget I had this meeting right now, especially on my first day?" Of course, this does nothing to help his clarity of mind, the relevance of his excuses, or his way of expressing them. In short, he feels like he's got everything wrong.

Our confused and judgmental relationship to our mistakes automatically leads to a feeling of guilt. We quickly and severely judge our misunderstandings, our blunders, and our partial and mistaken evaluations of things. We would so much like to be beyond reproach at all times. It's perfectly understandable, but is it possible?

Life—A Learning Process

If we consider ourselves as learners—in other words, if we realize that we cannot know everything, see everything, and understand everything at first glance; if we accept that our way of functioning only allows us to access our own representations of things, and if we assume that our relationship to others and to ourselves is emotional and therefore limited—then our relationship to making mistakes changes. Our life becomes a process of learning, discovery, and exploration.

Learning—building our stores of knowledge, developing the capacity to do and be different things—requires new ideas. It requires us to challenge our understanding and to readjust and deepen it. This can only occur through trial and error, through a process of learning that may be longer or shorter and more or less fruitful. It especially means learning to change our emotional reactions, to become familiar with our way of functioning, and to reconsider our partial and limiting representations. This learning can only be the result of patient and kind training.

Any learning process naturally and inevitably includes mistakes. How indeed could we learn without making mistakes? We can consider that learning means trying. Trying to understand; pushing ourselves to accomplish something; attempting to integrate something. This process cannot happen without imperfection, imprecision, distraction or mess-ups.

Thomas Edison said, "I have not failed. I have just found ten thousand ways that won't work!"[6]

Nelson Mandela similarly stated, "I never lose. I either win or learn."[7]

If we do not make mistakes, it means we already know what we need to—the necessary knowledge is already present. However, we always have more to learn—be it on an intellectual, relational, emotional, or cultural level. Indeed, it is our encounters with our own errors that allow us to progress. We learn from our misunderstandings, at least we do if we have a healthy relationship with making mistakes. There are several ways to learn from our errors and, likewise, several criteria in order to do so.

The Criteria for Evaluation

Different criteria allow us to evaluate an error, whether consciously or not. For example, in a friendship, one person may

---

6   Garson O'Toole, "I Have Gotten a Lot of Results. I Know Several Thousand Things that Won't Work," Quote Investigator, July 31, 2012, https://quoteinvestigator.com/2012/07/31/edison-lot-results/.

7   Text source unknown.

need a lot of expressions and gestures showing their care while the other person may not be able to show friendship in this way. One person may rely on little notes, phone calls, or consistent time spent together to feel that a friendship is alive, while the other person can only conceive of friendship as a profound connection without any special related expression. Seeing a friend again after months or even years apart and feeling as if they had just said goodbye the day before is one way of experiencing friendship.

These differences can lead one person or the other to question what mistakes they have made that led to not receiving what they expected from the other.

Since childhood, Jenny has always felt that if you love someone, you tell them. However, her father is a reserved man with little inclination toward outward signs of tenderness and has always been silent about his feelings toward her. Jenny thinks that her father doesn't love her or doesn't love her enough. Her father is now elderly and reaching the end of his life, yet he continues to keep his distance. Jenny dreams of one thing—hearing him say "I love you" before he dies. While this is certainly a legitimate wish, it is one that is impossible for her father to fulfill. He does not know how to speak his feelings aloud. He is unable to express his love in words. Despite this, he has showed Jenny how much he cares for her throughout her life by supporting her and helping her. He doesn't need words to say that he loves her. Nonetheless, Jenny suffers from his silence. For her, gestures are not enough. She doesn't feel that they are sufficient to show her that her father loves her. She needs words. Because this need goes unsatisfied, she concludes that she is not lovable—that no one could really love her because her own father does not say that he loves her.

Similar to this, we all have a representation of what should happen for everything to turn out okay—in terms of our relationships and also in terms of our vision of ourselves. We may be seduced by a certain type of personality.

For example, That Guy is cheerful, full of energy, and everyone likes being around him—at least that's how I perceive him. I, on the other hand, am shy, reserved, and have difficulty being outgoing.

Or instead, This Person is easygoing and rarely gets angry, whereas impatience and frustration regularly get the better of me. When we compare our own representation of ourself to an idealized other, we come out lacking. All of this occurs on the basis of unclear representations that we have not necessarily verified.

The feeling of error can also be tied to limited understanding of a situation. For example, I may have the impression that someone, let's call her Sara, doesn't do what she should because she's afraid and lacks self-confidence. For her part, Sara chooses not to act because she feels that the right circumstances for acting appropriately aren't present. Without considering Sara's motivation, it is an error on my part to judge her behavior as inappropriate simply because she doesn't act when I think she should.

These evaluation errors are common and sometimes lead us to react in a way that is out of step with the situation, which then generates further blunders—potential sources of feelings of guilt.

Clementine is a reserved young woman who dreams of meeting her Prince Charming. She imagines a kind and serious man, not necessarily Adonis nor a millionaire, but a reliable and honest person who she can build a life with. Of course, there's Freddie who's clearly expressed his interest in her, but he seems a bit shallow. He jokes around a lot and goes out often with friends. She thinks he's not serious enough. He doesn't fit her criteria. However, if one looks closer, Freddie is very committed to his professional life as well as being sincere and loyal. His spontaneity and liveliness are an obstacle for Clementine, who is fooled by appearances and stuck in her representations. Harsh judgment arises, "It's not okay to act like that!" Later, she'll learn that her indifference and her judgment hurt Freddie, and she'll be angry with herself for not having been able to see him for who he was.

Our emotional, afflictive relationship to situations is another important source of making mistakes. We are completely capable of developing great jealousy toward someone in our lives just based on a feeling. Or we might feel attacked and react with anger toward what seems to us to be someone else's bad attitude, while the other person felt they were simply being awkward. We've all experienced these situations—most visible when others misinterpret our own attitudes!

As we discussed, our view of a situation is always limited by our representations, and instead of judging ourselves or judging others, we can try to become aware of our limited perception. This source of error is the direct consequence of our way of functioning.

Numerous criteria for evaluation are based on culture, education, sexual identity, beliefs, ethical choices, etc. Let's look at a few examples.

In general, in the West, we seek out relationships based on honesty and directness. We place importance on telling the truth about who we are and what we do. Meanwhile, in certain countries in Asia, it is preferable to take care that another person does not lose face. Respecting others' reputations and dignity is at the heart of interactions, even at the risk of leaving out part of the truth. This can be misinterpreted by Westerners, as is true for the opposite.

Another criterion is that of language. For some people, swear words are inadmissible and for others they are a way to embellish their language. An even more extreme example is the very coded language of teenagers, which can feel aggressive to others though it is simply slang used by a group trying to define itself. In all the different circles of society, language trends are conventions that allow individuals to feel like part of a group. The need for recognition and belonging is essential for self-esteem, and feeling excluded from a group can generate feelings of guilt.

Beliefs—whose relevance we have not always examined—also condition our relationship to what is right and not right. Though today these representations have come into question, only recently a woman was always supposed to be reserved, maternal, and gentle, while a man needed to be strong and protective. Likewise, little boys were not supposed to cry and always played with cars or played sports, while little girls dressed in pink and played with dolls. Fortunately, some of these cultural representations have disappeared, but many have been replaced by others. Today, a woman should be active and sporty with a professional life, while also being gentle and maternal.

We can see that these ideas are in movement and ever changing—subject to the culture of the day. Meanwhile, they contribute to our evaluations on a more or less conscious level.

There is another deeply rooted belief that we hold to even as we can observe examples of its opposite quite regularly: there is an age for death and an age at which it is not normal to die. This leads to a feeling of injustice that causes us to look for someone to blame, regardless of the circumstances of death.

Here are a few more examples: If someone never talks in meetings, it must mean they have nothing to say, or maybe they are simple or incompetent. On the other hand, someone outgoing and cultured who easily speaks up is doubtless self-absorbed and simply showing off how much they know. Though these images are caricatures, we can find value judgments based on this type of unfounded belief in our relationships with others.

Caution! Let's not judge ourselves. Instead, let us simply observe our shortcomings with kindness so that we can patiently transform them.

Ethical Choices

We have chosen other criteria consciously—our ethical choices. These reference points guide us closer to correct action. In all religious and spiritual traditions, there is an ethical code that allows us to evaluate our actions with greater awareness. However, an ethical code can only exist in the context of a perspective—a view; a goal to cultivate and achieve. There are three possible approaches.

First—and this is often our motivation starting out—we want

to feel better. We also would like to be more available for the people around us and to cultivate the means to naturally become more useful in our environment. Another way to say this is—as Lama Jigme Rinpoche[8] puts it—that we want to be a good person and to cultivate appropriate ethics. This motivation allows us to have a better experience of the world and to feel more at ease with our way of functioning by cultivating the mind's inherent qualities and becoming less subject to our afflictions.

Here is another perspective: the Buddha shows us that our way of functioning cannot bring us lasting happiness. His teachings allow us to apply the means to liberate ourselves from suffering and its causes. He called this individual liberation. This path combines meditation and ethics and results in the realization of the emptiness of self—of identification with the five aggregates.

Here is a final approach: once we are aware of our suffering and its causes, the Buddha invites us to widen our vision to include the suffering of all beings. Then, we wish to commit to the path of the bodhisattvas and the achievement of the dual benefit—our own and that of others. This is the *Mahayana* path, or that of the Great Vehicle. It is the path that leads to Buddhahood—liberation from suffering and complete accomplishment of all of the mind's essential qualities.

---

8   Lama Jigme Rinpoche is the spiritual director of Dhagpo Kagyu Ling and an accomplished teacher of the Kagyü lineage.

This practice consists in cultivating a state of mind of kindness and compassion toward all beings and in developing an ever more lucid awareness of our way of functioning. Then, thanks to training in ethical action, meditation, and discernment, the veils that hinder clarity of mind dissipate little by little.

The basis of Buddhist ethics can be summed up in this short sentence, "Do not cause harm, and cultivate what is beneficial." Do not be harmful toward oneself or others—not only in a specific situation but also in the long term by becoming aware of the consequences of our actions.

This is not always simple because it is easier to be aware of consequences that are immediately visible than on their impact on our minds, which records and integrates our emotional responses, thus nurturing our habitual tendencies. For example, if I'm in the habit of reacting to any unpleasant situation with anger, this tendency will grow stronger each time I react this way. By contrast, if I become aware of the unhappiness this brings about for myself and those around me, I will be able to change my behavior little by little and progressively lessen the strength of this tendency.

The Buddha's teaching offers ethical reference points to help us develop an appropriate attitude; for example, not using our speech to deceive others, not taking what is not given, and being careful not to use hurtful or unkind words. These guidelines all help us toward this same goal: not causing harm and cultivating what is beneficial for all beings' happiness.

Making Mistakes as a Learning Process

Mistakes are an unavoidable part of the act of learning and in life in general. If we already know something, there is no learning, and therefore no mistakes. If we don't know, then there are no mistakes either because we are still in the process of learning. Even though at times we may think that not knowing is not an excuse, seeing our mistakes allows us to identify our shortcomings and weaknesses. When we are learning, our mistakes reveal what we need to work on and develop.

A mistake can lead to an impasse or, on the contrary, it can be creative and eye opening. Mistakes can be detrimental or helpful. Either way, they get our attention and cause us to ask questions. Mistakes show us which path to follow or adjust or give up. François Gervais[9] says, "Mistakes have always been the greatest teachers." We have something to learn from our mistakes. Therefore, it is pointless to consider them failures.

Without necessarily realizing it, we are always seeking perfection—a perfect action. Without being fully conscious of it, we think we know what we need to do, how to do it, and what result

---

9   Professor Emeritus of François Rabelais University in Tours, France.

we will get—and if things don't go as planned, we feel as if we've done something wrong, an obvious source of experiencing guilt. If we weren't the ones who have done something wrong, then it was someone else, everyone else, who led us astray. Thus, the vicious circle of unhappiness, loss of confidence in ourselves, and lack of trust in others continues.

A self-critical relationship to making mistakes is a key part of feeling guilty. If, by contrast, we consider mistakes to be new discoveries and an integral part of the process of creation and knowledge, then they become our greatest allies. We could say, "My screw-ups are the reason I grow!"

In general, we tend to consider any situation from our own point of view, colored by a relatively fixed vision of what it should be. Here, the idea is to reconsider the situation and explore its potential with healthy curiosity. What could I learn from this situation? What haven't I seen yet?

Exploring the unseen—unknown—and daring to take a fresh look at a situation creates space. Considering the different parameters involved and the various implications of a situation allows us to see that every situation is a composite of many different elements, which allows us to become aware of interdependence in a more productive way.

Making Mistakes as a Source of Discovery

Here is another, more surprising aspect of making mistakes: certain errors in the course of scientific research can lead to further discoveries, which is known as serendipity.[10]

From Fleming's discovery of penicillin to Post-It Notes with the development of rubber vulcanization along the way, events that were initially errors have punctuated the history of research and scientific discovery.

Alexander Fleming came back from vacation to find that a Petri dish of staphylococcus culture he hadn't cleaned before departing had been invaded by mold. He observed that the bacteria in contact with the mold was dead. Thus, an important discovery was born from negligence and—following development by other, subsequent researchers—it healed a great number of people thanks to the creation of penicillin.

The accidental discovery of a glue that didn't stick later gave birth to Post-It Notes. This glue—initially considered greasy and barely usable—found an unexpected utility on the little sticky papers now used all over the world.

Similarly, Charles Goodyear accidentally dropped a mix of rubber and sulfur onto a hot stove. When the mixture caught

---

10   Serendipity, sometimes called accidental discovery, originally referred to an unexpected or accidental scientific discovery or technical invention that came about from lucky circumstances and often in the course of research on another topic.

fire, he immediately threw the whole thing into the snow. Once cooled, the rubber was completely transformed. It was still elastic and waterproof, but it had also become heat-resistant and easy to work with. The important discovery of vulcanized rubber contributed to the develop of automobiles, among other things—and all this based on a blunder, a mistake!

Wrongdoing or Mistake

The idea of wrongdoing is more serious than that of making mistakes and involves a different field of meaning, though we often associate these two notions.

The idea of wrongdoing generally relates to a failure to uphold a promise, a transgression of moral law, to religious directives, and in this case specifically the notion of sin as expressed in Catholicism, for example. Lying, disrespecting one's parents, and nurturing envy or gluttony are all among the types of behavior considered sins and subject to condemnation.

On a legal level, wrongdoing refers to an infraction, offense, or crime such as larceny, murder, etc. This can also refer to a percentage of or full responsibility for an accident. It also includes carelessness and negligence—oversights that can constitute an infraction—as in the case of breaking traffic law.

How many lapses of vigilance while driving are due to impatience or the desire to outmaneuver or pass someone else? How many accidents are the result of unconscious overexhaustion or excessive drinking? How many occur due to inattention because we know the road by heart?

All of these infractions relate to factual guilt and may or may not be accompanied by feelings of guilt.

The Buddhist perspective offers another vision of the notion of wrongdoing. Any mistakes we make, even if they lead to wrongdoing, are rooted in our self-centered, emotional way of functioning.

Not respecting a law or transgressing a taboo is the result of incomplete vision conditioned by our imprecise representations. Our seriously afflicted means of acquiring knowledge leads to inappropriate behavior due to our fascination with our attraction to, or rejection of, certain situations. We act under the influence of the afflictions without great awareness of the repercussions for ourselves and others.

Becoming aware of the consequences of our actions means having a correct vision of the situations we encounter and clarity that we unfortunately often lack.

This explanation is not intended to excuse everything or to minimize actions that have been carried out. The point is to understand what animates us, what motivates us. Our endless search for wellbeing and pleasure leads us to commit harmful actions without realizing it in the moment. Quite often, it is only upon seeing the negative consequences that we become aware of our mistakes.

When certain consequences bring us or others suffering, we then experience strong and harsh—even uncompromising— judgment that reinforces the feeling of guilt. However, if the exterior consequences are minimal and no one was around to witness our wrongdoing, it seems much less serious to us.

Buddhist ethics invites us to become aware of the harmful consequences for others and also the negative effects on our own minds.

Buddhist Practice and Guilt

Looking at Our Way of Functioning

While the Buddha taught a universal view, that view is different from our own culture. Before encountering the Buddha's teaching, we believe in the reality of what we perceive. We are certain that phenomena truly exist and that we are each truly a unique, individual, and independent person—and that others are as well.

The Dharma leads us to question these certainties and—as part of this—invites us to reflect on the meaning of the teachings. However, we cannot understand a new vision on the basis of our previous knowledge. We need time to reflect and, little by little, open to the Buddhist view.

This is not really a problem. We cannot force the mind. Better understanding can only occur progressively, and yet we so wish that this training could yield rapid results! This is not possible. First, we must receive the teaching from someone able to properly transmit it, and next we need to take the time to integrate the meaning of what we have heard by reflecting and assimilating it through our own experience.

Then, there will come a time when we acquire a certain intellectual understanding, but we struggle to apply it. Even though we are aware of anger arising, and even though we know it is harmful for ourselves and others, we still let ourselves get carried away by the current of emotion.

Being able to see and failing to not follow the emotional movements of our minds can become a source of guilty feelings. We can see how quickly self-judgment of our imperfections arises, "I'll never get it! I'm so lame. If only I could react differently. I wish I were more patient," etc.

Our view of ourselves is often harsh and uncompromising, which generates even more suffering and dissatisfaction. Feelings of guilt only reinforce our afflictions. They rob us of our clarity and discernment. Feeling guilty limits our ability to take responsibility because it causes us to grasp onto our own idea of what should have been without allowing us to relate to what was.

Of course, we are aware that remaining calm with a clear and kind view of the situation is the key to facing our way of functioning in a more productive manner. But we are often trapped in our representations of what we wish we could be here and now without managing to consider that simply accepting what we are is essential to clarifying the mind. Simply and clearly observing allows us to embrace our dysfunction for what it is—material for transformation, rather than an obstacle.

If we are simply aware of the situation—of what is—clarity of mind will spontaneously reveal itself with habit because it is already present. It is useless to wait yearningly or hope to be able to grasp it.

Meditation and Guilt

Training in meditation consists in familiarizing ourself with the mind's movements without following or rejecting them so that we are no longer dependent on them. However, we cannot prevent ourselves from spontaneously commenting and judging our experiences, especially our difficulty remaining focused. We can even go so far as to guilt trip ourselves if what we experience does not match our idea of meditation. These judgments generate a feeling of being wrong that undermines our confidence and self-esteem. We have a lot of difficulty when we do not obtain immediate results that conform to our representations of good meditation.

By trying to encounter the mind as we imagine it, we miss out on the mind as it is. Instead, we look at our way of functioning based on the representation we have of meditation. It is difficult to simply look without judgment at what is for what it is—in other words, movements, thoughts, emotions, and commentary.

Often, we imagine meditation as a state of calm without thoughts or emotion and, because of this, we force ourselves not to think. It is impossible to bridle the mind's movements. They are the expression of its creativity and inherent to its functioning. Instead, the point is to simply be conscious of the mind's movements and train ourselves in not following them and coming back to the breath.

We may likewise think that we should have experiences—moments of clarity—but we are looking so hard for these moments that we block them. Moments of clarity can only occur with a calm, relaxed mind free from seeking. Just be there. This is not the easiest for us. We are more often involved in mental or physical activity than in welcoming what is happening now, in the moment.

Contrary to all logic, we sometimes think that the more we perceive the tumult of thoughts, emotions, and sensations during meditation, the more our meditation is incorrect. However, if we look closer, we were present for all these movements, and we came back to the breath again and again[11].

---

11   To delve deeper into this subject, read Lama Jigme Rinpoche, *A Path of Wisdom* (La Remuée: Rabsel Editions, 2012).

Nonetheless, we may tell ourselves that it was a bad meditation because our mind was agitated for the whole time. What if awareness of agitation is the very expression of a mind in meditation?

In the process of meditation, it is just as important to notice our agitation and the different thoughts that arise as it is to remain focused on the support of the breath. There is nothing to add or remove from our experience. We train ourselves to become familiar with and accept what is there—to simply observe and come back to the support without grasping or rejecting.

We dream of being calm with a clear and peaceful mind. This is natural, but, in order to achieve this, we need to learn how to be in contact with the mind's agitation, its creativity, and its afflictive functioning—so that little by little we no longer depend on it, and we can discover another means of knowing free from attachment to appearances and afflictions.

Meditation is a natural process. There is no need to trick or force the mind. It suffices to leave the mind in its natural state with great awareness. We must certainly not expect immediate results. The results will appear with time. Let us simply be natural and experience the situation as it is in the moment.[12]

_____

12 Excerpt from an oral teaching by Lama Jigme Rinpoche at Dhagpo Kagyu Ling.

Guilt from a Relative Point of View

Talking about guilt means talking about suffering. Guilt is a heavy, painful, hobbling, and even paralyzing feeling. It conditions our relationship to ourselves and others. It has an impact on self-confidence and, therefore, self-esteem.

But what guilt are we talking about? Is it the result of a mistake, of wrongdoing, or is it guilt born of a confused feeling that we did not do or say what we should have done or said? We can distinguish two main types of guilt—factual guilt and the feeling of guilt.

Factual Guilt

Committing a crime, breaking the law, running a red light—all of these things involve our responsibility—our guilt in relation to society. Most of the time this guilt is evident, even if it is sometimes contested or shared.

Diverse stories from the news give numerous examples of this. Whether people act based on greed, jealousy, or anger—whatever the underlying motivation—they are fully and completely responsible for their transgressions, even if we can find extenuating circumstances.

Factual guilt leads us to face our actions in terms of legality and society. It may or may not be accompanied by a feeling of guilt—that painful feeling of smallness, the sensation of not being able to face the situation.

All of us have likely infringed upon the traffic code at some point or another without any consequence other than being outside the law. Going a little over the speed limit, hitting the accelerator at a yellow light, getting a little pushy about who has the right of way, etc.—so many normal, minor transgressions. If a traffic cop surprised us, we'd surely try to negotiate! It is not certain that we would recognize our error straightaway; anger and frustration at being caught in the act would likely predominate. It is not certain that feelings of guilt would be present for each of us in this situation. It is also not certain that we truly take fully responsibility. A few justifications would allow us to get away with our heads high or we might even question the validity of the traffic laws.

For some people, however, getting caught in the act is by nature guilt-inducing even if the transgression is minor. For others—for their own reasons—this feeling does not occur even if their actions have harmful consequences for others. The feeling of guilt is not accessible for everyone, while for some individuals even their factual guilt is contestable from their own point of view.

We will essentially focus on the feeling of guilt in this reflection because, while factual guilt is beyond argument, feelings of guilt are much less so. What's more, we can remedy them.

Feeling Guilty

Even if the feeling of guilt is inherent in our self-centered way of functioning—the process of endless identification in search of balance and happiness—it is nonetheless partly conditioned by our culture.

Quite often, we refer to Judeo-Christian culture as being at the root of our relationship to guilt. Perhaps it participated in reinforcing this relationship, but this culture is not required to incite guilt in us. Many non-religious families also suffer from feelings of guilt.

More generally, Western culture preaches the quest for perfection—academic success, personal success, etc. Wanting a life that conforms to some kind of ideal and does not match our daily life can lead us to experience this disparity as a failure.

Depending on our relationship to making mistakes, feelings of guilt arise spontaneously when we have the impression of not being good enough, of being wrong, of having screwed up in this or that situation, etc. Whether we are correct or not in our reading of the situation, we feel as though we have done something wrong, even immoral—that we did or said something reprehensible and unacceptable to ourselves or others. An irrepressible and sometimes devastating emotional current then wells up within us.

The Roots of Feeling Guilty

We can often find one of the roots of guilt in our childhood. Remember how important it is for a child to grow up in a stable environment, where the feeling of being loved and considered provides stability. Yet all the love parents can offer is not necessarily enough to develop healthy self-esteem that limits the tendency to feel guilty.

A child who arrives in the world is not a blank page. Children arrive with their tendencies—their emotional register—foundations that allow them to establish their own representation of themselves and the world, as well as of the individuals around them. As such, they will react to their emotional environment based on what has been accumulated in their mind.

This obviously doesn't negate the parents' responsibility, but it would be incorrect to think that their behavior concerning the child is the sole origin of the child's difficulties. The meeting of a great number of causes and circumstances mold an individual.

Furthermore, family events can likewise be upsetting for children. The arrival of brothers and sisters, their place in the family, the parents' separation, or the loss of a loved one can have an impact on the child's experience.

Luke is the firstborn—the child his parents so longed for and to whom they devote all their attention. For three years, the family has revolved around him. Then his little brother Julian arrives—no less longed for and no less loved. For Luke, the baby has stolen his place and, what's more, as the big brother, he has to be sweet and attentive to his little brother despite the fact that he's mainly feeling resentment. Thus, jealousy arises leading to a loss of confidence and especially to a feeling of rivalry that robs Luke of his inner resources. Likewise, it's also not easy for Julian to find his place. Depending on his own tendencies, he may try to impose himself with force and anger or, on the contrary, he might try to shrink himself so as not to provoke his brother's impatience.

We can easily observe these altogether ordinary situations that influence a child's experience and affect their capacity to face the situations they encounter as adults.

Our educational system likely contributes to reinforcing feelings of guilt. The evaluation of schoolwork depends less on what the student did correctly than on the number of mistakes. Academic assessment involves one's failures more than one's successes. Furthermore, children do not have the same needs in terms of the amount of time necessary to integrate new information. Some go more slowly, while others assimilate new things quickly and get bored. Some are daydreamers. Some only have a limited ability to focus.

Nonetheless, an adult perspective—that of their parents or teachers—on their rhythm and mistakes has an impact on a child's experience. Depending on that adult perspective, mistakes can be seen as an obstacle to success or as a natural part of the learning process.

Feelings of guilt also stem from lack of self-confidence and low self-esteem. Whether it is due to the circumstances we encounter, a feeling of constant criticism, or a sensitive time in our lives, most of us struggle with our self-esteem. Our own perspective on our shortcomings and weaknesses, along with others' judgment—or at least our perception of it—influences the way we look at ourselves.

What makes up positive self-esteem? Looking at ourselves with kindness is one important foundation. This allows us to see and accept what we truly are—beings endowed with intrinsic positive qualities and inner wealth—resources that we can rely on. At the same time, we are beings whose emotional way of functioning limits and conditions our relationship to phenomena—regardless of what they are. In addition, another important element is self-confidence. This inner assuredness requires cultivation and allows us to rely on our own abilities and competence to accomplish things and to succeed when we try new things despite our limits.

Thus, self-esteem is made up of the ability to look at our way of functioning with kindness, which helps have a clear vision of ourselves. This, in turn, positively influences self-confidence, which allows us to act without fear of failure or other's judgment.

When these three elements are in balance, positive self-esteem is most stable and less easily shaken in situations of failure or error. Therefore, feelings of guilt have much less power over us. By contrast, critical self-judgment and a lack of self-confidence automatically lead to feelings of guilt.

Very often it is difficult to accept our inner emotional waves and admit in the moment that our vision is limited, incomplete, and colored by our tendencies—and that our understanding is conditioned by our way of functioning—without feeling invalidated. We want so much to be right! We wish so hard that we could not mess up, not make mistakes!

This feeling is quite understandable, but it is not our current reality. Our relationship to ourselves and others is distorted by our way of apprehending based on representations. This is not a real problem; the crucial point is to see it and accept it in order to be able to change it little by little.

As we can only change what we see and accept, we should rejoice in seeing. Obviously, the point is not to rejoice in seeing our weaknesses, but to rejoice in having seen them, because a weakness that we have seen is a potential strength.

Quite often, we underestimate the power of rejoicing, of rejoicing in having seen. Not only does this bring levity to our practice, but it is also a solid foundation for cultivating patience, joyful effort, and kindness—states of mind that are favorable for applying the practice of the three trainings—ethics, meditation, and discernment.

Guilt and Afflictions

The experience of feeling guilty reinforces confusion and prevents us from having a clear vision of the situation we are in due to the emotional upheaval it generates. A multitude of contradictory thoughts collide and fuel painful suffering. *I should have; I shouldn't have; if I had known,* etc. are only so many recurring thoughts that can act like a knife in the gut, incessantly reminding us of our mistake.

These thoughts are a flow of emotions that arise and, depending on the context, become more or less overwhelming. Feelings of guilt often appear at the same time as other afflictions. A veritable cocktail of emotion invades us. Let us consider a few examples.

The feeling of guilt associated with aversion and anger: when things don't go as planned—as we intended—they become an obstacle to our feeling of wellbeing.

It's a fine summer day, and we have been planning a picnic for weeks and looking forward to the joy of spending time with our loved ones. Everything is in order, and we've thought of all the details. Everything except the unpredictable! The unpredictable shows up in the form of one friend cancelling, another having car trouble, and a third being home sick with the flu. All that's left is frustration. Anger—that unwise advisor—leads us to pick up the phone and tell everyone how we feel. "Nothing ever goes the way I want." Barely listening to others' explanations, we get caught up in reproach and hurtful words. After the fact, we realize that our reaction was excessive and unfair, and we find ourselves overwhelmed with guilt.

The famous guilt-inducing *I should have* that tortures us following what we deem a failure is a feeling of guilt associated with regret in its harmful form.

I should have seen that my behavior would make her break up with me, he tells himself. *I should have gone out with the guys less often. I should have seen that I left her by herself too often. I should have seen that I wasn't giving her enough attention. It's my fault that it's over.*

I should have told my caring and reserved father how much I loved him. I should have thanked him for everything he gave me. Now that he's no longer here, I can see how much my seeming indifference must have made him suffer.

I should have taken better care of myself. I shouldn't have gotten carried away with so much excess. I should have gone to see the doctor sooner. Now here I am, sick, and the prognosis is not great. My kids are still so young to face all this.

Guilt associated with fear of being the root of other's suffering; fear of the consequences of our way of seeing, doings things, and reacting to the different circumstances we encounter—this feeling can be nearly constant, or it can be connected with certain situations and issues.

Marie had a fight with one of her sisters and feels responsible for it. Now she doesn't know how to reach out or fix things in the face of her sister's obstinate silence. A few weeks later, her sister calls to make peace and invites her for a girl's day out of shopping. Marie already has plans that day, and she can't cancel them. What to do? Should she risk disappointing her sister? Rescheduling her plans is out of the question. Yet she can't imagine hurting her sister again. Guilt and fear paralyze Marie and prevent her from seeing any alternatives, which causes to her to give an inept response to her sister's olive branch.

Attachment to our self-image in conjunction with guilt can lead to feelings of remorse.

Even though I knew it wasn't right to go along with criticizing so and so, I listened and nodded and maybe even encouraged it to avoid getting called-out by my colleagues. It was more important to me to look out for my reputation than to stick to my own ethics, which creates feelings of guilt and remorse now that I see it.

Attachment in conjunction with jealousy is also an amplifier of suffering when connected with feelings of guilt. How often are we overtaken by jealousy when one of our relationships may escape us? It is even more painful if we feel responsible for the situation.

George's partner tried very hard to get him to join her for a weekend yoga retreat. But George doesn't really like yoga and prefers doing things he enjoys, like staying at home peacefully and gardening. His partner headed to the retreat on her own, and on Saturday evening she calls him to share her enthusiasm and especially her pleasure at meeting another participant—a guy—who she can't stop talking about. George is worried and wonders if it would have been better if he'd gone with her. He keeps imagining everything that could happen in his absence. Guilt and jealousy will torture him through Sunday evening, when he will anxiously await her return.

We can see how feelings of guilt can manifest on so many occasions—with or without an obvious reason or objective responsibility. In some situations of abuse or assault, we cannot help feeling guilty even though we know perfectly well that we are the victim. Contrary to all logic, we continue to think with a certain degree of confusion that we should have defended ourselves, run, not let it happen—even though we couldn't in the moment! Being a victim, knowing it, and feeling guilty can also generate further guilt. *I should get out of this way of thinking*, without considering that willpower is not enough. Some work is often necessary and even crucial to becoming free from this type of guilt.

Buddhism and Guilt

In his teaching, the Buddha focused on essential aspects of our way of functioning that hinder clarity of mind: the confusion or cognitive error that prevents us from seeing things as they are; tendencies or *nyeunmong*, translated as disturbing emotions or afflictions.

The teachings emphasize the five afflictions most responsible for obstacles so that we can recognize them and train ourselves to no longer be subject to their afflictive power. These five afflictions are desire-attachment or appropriation, aversion, mental opacity, pride, and jealousy. The feeling of guilt is not considered an affliction in and of itself, but rather an amalgam of several afflictions. The first four emotional occurrences listed here make up the basis for the feeling of guilt.

Our way of functioning leads us to become attached to what pleases us, reassures us, comforts us, and is convenient for us—everything that we are sure of. One of the sites of attachment that is among the most difficult to identify is our attachment to our representations. Most of the time, we are certain that what we have seen or understood in a situation is the truth—the reality. Feelings of guilt reinforce this mechanism because they lead to being stuck in our experience of what happened, exaggerated by the sentiment of wrongdoing.

Due to our attachment, we distance ourselves from and reject everything that brings instability or is unpleasant or disturbing. Occurrences of aversion generate anger, hatred, hostility, impatience, etc.

As for mental opacity, it allows us to see solely our own version of reality and, in consequence, there are many aspects of reality that we do not take into account. This blindness is considered an affliction because it veils and disturbs what we perceive, while also partly conditioning our reaction.

Pride is perceiving ourself as an individual being and deeply grasping to a superior or insignificant self-image. This affliction expresses as pretention and arrogance but also poor self-esteem or an inferiority complex.

The few afflictions identified here are constantly active. They are part of our mode of acquiring knowledge, but many other harmful states of mind are also active. We only know ourselves, others, phenomena, and situations through these filters that mark our understanding, coloring our reactions and leaving a record in our minds that will continue to condition our perceptions.

Causes and Conditions

Our mode of acquiring knowledge does not allow us to consider different aspects of reality—such as that all phenomena are composite, interdependent, and impermanent.

Nothing exists on its own in an autonomous and lasting way. Everything depends on the coming together of multiple causes and circumstances that we have little control over.

As we saw, guilt arises during an after-the-fact reading of a situation that we retrospectively evaluate as being inadequate and that we always express in the conditional. *I should have seen, known, shouldn't have said or done; if I had known.*

Understanding the use of the conditional is doubtless an interesting topic of reflection. Using this grammatical tense shows that all of the conditions were not present for things to go another way. Every situation, whatever it is, is the result of multiple causes and circumstances. The expression *if I had known* shows that I didn't know, and yet, my representations lead me to think that I should have known!

In his book *What Makes You Not a Buddhist*, Dzongsar Jamyang Khyentse evokes the multitude of causes and conditions necessary to cook a hard-boiled egg. A chicken, of course, but also a pot of water, the flame, etc., up to the tiniest detail. He says,

> When all the innumerable causes and conditions come together, and there is no obstacle of interruption, the result is inevitable. [...] Like the egg, *all* phenomena are the product of myriad components, and therefore they are variable. Nearly all of these myriad components are beyond our control, and for that reason they defy our expectations.[13]

Thus, we can understand that despite our will, our wishes, our expectations, we cannot believe that everything will happen the way we want it to. The attachment that we cultivate for situations and relationships automatically generates expectations, many of which cannot be satisfied. Far from being a sign of our shortcomings, the disappointment we experience reveals the irrelevance of our expectations, which do not take into account numerous parameters over which we have no control.

Viewing disappointment as revealing our expectations is surely the most productive way to approach the reflection concerning everything we *should* have seen or known. Negative judgment and guilt cut us off from an important resource—the

---

13   Dzongsar Jamyang Khyentse, *What Makes You Not a Buddhist* (Boston: Shambala Publications, Inc., 2008), 24.

opportunity to learn from a disappointing situation.

Disappointment is a good sign of basic intelligence. It cannot be compared to anything else: it is so sharp, precise, obvious and direct. If we can open, then we suddenly begin to see that our expectations are irrelevant compared with the reality of the situations we are facing. This automatically brings a feeling of disappointment.

Disappointment is the best chariot to use on the path of the dharma. It does not confirm the existence of our ego and its dreams.[14]

The Afflictions of Feeling Guilty

Guilt is a complex feeling—the result of several afflictions. Let us start with an example to consider the Buddhist view of this feeling.

Kristie wakes up a little late in the morning. She didn't sleep well and struggles to get out of bed, and, on top of that, there are no more coffee filters! The day doesn't start out great, but it's no big deal. Traffic is heavier later in the morning, and she gets in late to the office. Her impatience is starting to rise more seriously. She's not very chatty with her coworkers when she arrives, and they give her a hard time for being grumpy, which only makes her mood worse. The day goes on in the same vein. By the time she

---

14 Chogyam Trungpa, *Cutting Through Spiritual Materialism* (Boston: Shambhala Publications, Inc., 2002), 25.

gets home, her stress is at its maximum, and the first slightly unpleasant exchange makes her explode. Her boyfriend asks innocently, "What's for dinner?" It's the straw that breaks the camel's back. "Why is it always my job to figure out what's for dinner?" Obviously, the conflict heats up and both parties retreat in frustration. Of course, Kristie is upset with herself and feels guilty. *I shouldn't have gotten mad*, etc. without realizing the accumulated weight of the day's frustrations.

What afflictions are at play here, and how do they work?

In this context, attachment basically works in relation to representations. In the moment and from her point of view, Kristie is sure that her boyfriend is being demanding. He shouldn't have spoken to her like that.

However, considering the situation after the fact, Kristie is sure that it's her fault and that she shouldn't have gotten angry. The rejection of her own attitude and the mistake she made lead her to feel guilty.

Blinded by her contradictory feelings, Kristie doesn't take into account the build-up of frustration and stress throughout her day. The feeling of being in the wrong leads to overgeneralizing, to not seeing all of the elements of a situation. From this moment on, because Kristie feels at fault, guilt will color the relationship and condition her various reactions.

By the way, where do we get the idea that we are never supposed to mess up and never allowed to make mistakes? Looking at this, we can see the part that pride plays in feeling guilty. We don't want to face our limits or our errors. We reject our lack of clarity—we want so much to be perfect. This is thoroughly understandable but not very applicable based on our way of functioning.

From the perspective of the Dharma, we can understand the feeling of guilt as an amalgam of these four afflictions: attachment, aversion, mental opacity, and pride. Though our analysis of this example is somewhat artificial, it nevertheless allows us to reflect on various notions.

Understanding our mode of acquiring knowledge—in other words, our dependence on afflictions and lack of clarity in regard to our way of functioning—in conjunction with the application of Buddhist methods allows us to cultivate inner freedom little by little.

We foster this inner freedom using three trainings: training in ethics, meditation, and discernment. On the basis of ethics, we become aware of what we need to develop and what we need to give up, which allows us to cultivate the appropriate attitude. This doesn't remove the issue of the afflictions, but a process of clarification occurs progressively through meditation. Little by little, becoming familiar with the mind's movements—whether afflictions or thoughts—and training in not following them leads to greater clarity. By training in discernment, we allow for a deep knowledge of our way of functioning to arise. These trainings allow us to bring together favorable conditions for a meaningful life.

These three trainings mutually enrich each other, depend on each other, and develop in tandem. This allows us to progressively become able to identify the afflictions at work in our daily lives. Doing so then allows us to develop a greater capacity not to follow them.

This occurs by seeing what is happening for us—identifying anger, for example, accepting the disturbance of the emotional movement, and not following it. This is a daily form of training to apply progressively, without pressure, beginning with ordinary life situations where the stakes are low. For example, we can work on recognizing our impatient reaction when we are alone facing a situation that we cannot change, like being stuck at a red light when we're running late.

The same goes for all the afflictions. Little by little, these steps allow us to become less overwhelmed by the power of our emotions until we finally no longer depend on them. Furthermore, if we add rejoicing in what we have seen, we will be able to walk the path with greater levity.

Forgiveness and Regret

Forgiveness

Let us start with our culture, in which forgiveness is a response to guilt. Forgiving is not an easy thing to do. It requires truly questioning oneself and elicits the ability to show kindness and awareness.

There are many books on the topic[15]—and much reflection and advice on how to go about it. We will only cover a few aspects here.

Forgiveness does not mean forgetting, denying, or going back to the way things were before. The consequence of the mistake

---

15   Nicole Fabre, *Les Paradoxes du Pardon* [in French] (Paris: Éditions Albin Michel, 2007).

made leaves traces on our history—particularly when the act involves major physical or psychological suffering.

There are three types of forgiveness: forgiveness we ask for, forgiveness we give someone else, and forgiveness we give ourselves. All three types require kind awareness, understanding of the error committed, and the wish to repair the harm caused.

Concerning forgiveness to another or oneself, the first step is renouncing any wish for vengeance or self-punishment. Then comes recognition of the harm and the afflictions that it generated. It is important to be clear that understanding an aggressor—a necessary prerequisite for forgiveness—does not mean accepting, accepting everything. Understanding means not reducing a being to their actions.

Forgiveness is an act of generosity and trust that can be spoken and shared or accomplished in the secret space of one's own mind. Forgiving also does not mean continuing a relationship. Depending on the severity of the suffering caused, it may be preferable to cut all outer connection with the person responsible.

Regret

From the perspective of the Buddha's teaching, forgiveness brings up a crucial question. Doesn't it confirm the notion of wrongdoing and immorality? If I have to forgive, then somebody must have done something wrong or even immoral. In addition to forgiveness, Buddhist practice offers another remedy—awareness of the mistake made and the practice of regret concerning our own errors.

The notion of inherent immorality is not present in the Dharma. We have deduced that the notion of immorality connected to the idea of sin is the result of negative judgment of mistakes. What types of mistakes does this concern? This includes mistakes in understanding or evaluating as well as afflicted reactions, of course, but if we explore the basis for our mistakes in greater depth, it is the identification with the body and the mind that is the essential cause—the primary cause that automatically generates mistakes, dissatisfaction, suffering, etc.

The difficulties that we encounter are the natural result of our way of functioning, and it is important to understand the consequences of actions on our minds. Actions—both harmful and beneficial—leave imprints on our minds that generate future suffering or happiness. This is why training in ethics based on understanding of causality and founded on correct motivation is so important.

Knowing that we are stuck in this way of functioning and having observed our difficulty to transform it, we can understand and recognize that the same is true for all beings, as they are likewise conditioned by ignorance.

If we can understand this, what is there to forgive? This is a crucial point in the face of suffering caused by other people—or that seems so to us. *It's so-and-so's fault that I'm upset, unhappy, angry, etc.* This is a common vision, but is it correct?

If I am angry, I am the cause—the other person is merely the circumstance. No one other than myself can generate anger within me. Another person cannot make me mad. I make myself mad when I come into contact with them.

The affliction that arises within me is the result of my way of functioning. The speed at which I get carried away by anger, for example, clearly indicates my habit of reacting that way when I do not accept a situation.

I have no power—no control—over what happens outside my personal field of action, whether it's pleasant for me or not. I cannot change the situation as it presents itself, but I can change my relationship to the situation.

By training in meditation, we clarify our relationship to afflictions. By training in ethics, we reduce our harmful actions, and our beneficial states of mind increase. By training in discernment, we discover a heightened ability for reflection and a vaster capacity for knowledge and awareness.

The goal is to understand our way of functioning, to see both the harmful and beneficial aspects. The mind is endowed with immense positive qualities, including a capacity for awareness and knowledge whose potential we are mostly ignorant of. These qualities are already at work. We can see that we are capable of generosity, patience, kindness, and a certain discernment, but these qualities are limited by the process of identification that hinders and limits the mind's natural clarity.

If we understand our current limitations, if we accept them for what they are—impermanent yet powerful obstacles—if we consciously wish to free ourselves from them, and if we put into practice the methods proposed by the Buddha, there is no doubt that our minds will reveal their clarity to a greater and greater extent—clarity marked by compassion and wisdom.

Buddhism talks about fundamental kindness present in each individual. There is not, however, anything fundamentally negative in human beings. Each of us has the potential to follow the path of liberation at our own rhythm, according to the circumstances we encounter.

In his book *In Search of Wisdom*,[16] Matthieu Ricard writes,

[In the Buddhist tradition], there is no notion of original sin, no hereditary fault that could be interpreted as something wrong with you. There is only the effect of actions you have committed yourself in either a recent or distant past. Thus we only speak of personal responsibility and the possibility, which is always present, of amending one's conditions by avoiding the kinds of

---

16 Matthieu Ricard, Christophe André and Alexandre Jollien, *In Search of Wisdom: A Monk, a Philosopher, and a Psychiatrist on What Matters Most* (Louisville: Sounds True Inc., 2015).

mistakes made in the past. There is no inherited wrong that can be experienced as an injustice. There are only the results of the actions we have committed ourselves—in a near or distant past. Therefore, we only speak about personal responsibility and the ever-present possibility of remedying our condition by avoiding past errors. [...] Whatever the darkness of our actions, it is always possible to remedy them.

Learning to embrace our mistakes while being aware of their consequences and without judging them—or at least with awareness of and without following those judgments—is the requisite basis for cultivating regret. Sincere regret for being carried away again and again by our afflictions in conjunction with cultivating the means to get out of this way of functioning is a spiritual practice with the side effect of cutting off the roots of guilt. It consists in meaningful regret born from recognizing our errors without negative judgment and with kindness for ourselves.

When regret degenerates into guilt, it can lead to low self-esteem with its entourage of suffering. Another pitfall to watch out for is a form of complacence regarding our errors. The goal is to find the right attitude between a critical, judgmental view and a lax view that remains blind.

However, the spiritual practice of regret in no way negates the necessity of forgiving those who have hurt us—it is often socially and culturally necessary. Errors—both cognitive and afflictive—are unavoidable. They occur based on our imprecise, emotional representations, which keep us imprisoned in our own version of reality. This is true for all beings. If we understand and accept this, we can forgive because the other person needs us to. On the inside, we recognize their mistake, and on the outside, we forgive them.

Conclusion

Let's go over the key points of our reflection on feeling guilty. The essence is understanding our way of functioning and knowing that we can question it in order to free ourselves from it little by little. Contrary to what we believe, our way of functioning is not as fixed and determined as we perceive it to be. Therefore, we can work on it.

Another aspect of our reflection focuses on our relationship to error, which is a critical factor in the development of feelings of guilt. Do we consider ourselves to be students? Are we aware that we are in a phase of learning, of knowledge to discover and cultivate? Clarifying our relationship to error positively contributes to weakening our judgments and favors the transformation of guilt-inducing situations into opportunities to grow.

The foundation of Buddhist practice is the application of ethical discipline, which invites us to reduce our harmful actions and to cultivate beneficial states of mind. In light of the fact that any form of ethics is naturally in service of a goal or point of view, it is important to clarify our aspiration. What direction are we seeking with our work on feeling guilty? First, we need to determine our motivation as clearly as possible—and then to train in that motivation and deepen it. We saw that the Dharma offers several perspectives here.

One possibility is that we are aware of the suffering caused by our way of functioning, and we wish to cultivate beneficial relationships. Based on this, we take inspiration from humanism imbued with altruistic values and try to apply the methods to be a good, generous, and caring human being.

A second possibility is that we have seen the limits of our current way of functioning and wish to become free of it. In this case, we can engage in the path of individual liberation.

A third and final possibility is that we have seen that all beings wish for lasting happiness just as we do, and we have the profound wish to accomplish the dual benefit—our own and that of others. This motivation, called bodhicitta or enlightened mind,[17] is the vastest of the three perspectives and leads to full and perfect enlightenment—the state of Buddhahood.

"May all beings be separated from suffering and the causes of suffering.

May all beings know happiness and the causes of happiness."[18]

We train in meditation and discernment, and we rely on the resources that the Dharma offers. We patiently cultivate the means to accomplish the dual benefit. Based on this vast motivation, we develop the means to free ourselves from suffering.

Discernment means seeing things as they are in order to go beyond our limited and imprecise representations. Throughout the training, we progress from partial knowledge to vast knowledge.

Using the methods of the Buddha's teaching—particularly training in meditation—we clarify our relationship to the afflictions. Through this, we discover a heightened capacity for reflection and vaster discernment. Our vision of guilt naturally transforms, and we discover the resources to react in a relevant way to the situations of daily life.

---

17   To delve deeper into this subject, read Lama Jigme Rinpoche, *The Handbook of Ordinary Heroes: The Bodhisattvas' Way* (La Remuée: Rabsel Editions, 2016).

18   These are the first two of four lines of prayer known as the "The Four Immeasurables."

Acknowledgements

I would like to express my gratitude to the lamas who have guided me and continue to guide me on the Buddhist path: Lama Gendun Rinpoche, Lama Jigme Rinpoche, and all the masters who have illuminated my journey and who allow me to put the Buddha's teaching into practice with their teachings and wise counsel.

I would also like to particularly thank Lama Puntso, without whom this text would never have seen the light of day.

A big thank you to Christophe Fauré, a very dear friend, who wrote the preface. His competency in service of others and his availability for me are a warm and helpful source of support.

I would also like to thank all the people who allowed me to

limit the errors in this book through their encouragement and thoughtful advice.

Thank you to all those who shared their knowledge and experience. Thank you to all those who have allowed me to journey at their sides and who have enriched my life with their trust.

Publishing finished
in July 2021 by Pulsio
Publisher Number: 4018
Legal Deposit: July 2021
Printed in Bulgaria